COMBATTING THE EVIL EYE

COMBATTING THE EVIL EYE

EVIL EYE

Galina Krasskova

SANNGETALL PRESS

CONTENTS

*For my students, apprentices,
and all those who wish to learn*

Introduction

When I was asked to write the introduction to this book, I found myself wondering what I could contribute that had not already been covered within its pages. Drawn from a class Galina Krasskova originally taught several years ago, this information on dealing with the evil eye is as relevant and timely now as it ever has been. I am seeing more and more cases of it, and I often find myself pondering the collective wisdom of our ancestors in deterring it. It is so simple to avoid or block, that I wish everyone were taught these techniques as a matter of course.

It is well-known fact of psychotherapy that those emotions we refuse to deal with will, in time, find ways to leak out and affect our lives. The same thing happens with magic and with psi-gifts. Emotions are powerful; emotions are energy; and if we refuse to acknowledge and truly own that which we feel, the results can be destructive to ourselves, and sometimes—if we possess the right combination of talents—to others.

I had lunch with a colleague and friend once not too long ago and she told me a rather disturbing tale. She has been counseling a woman that I shall call M. for a couple of years now on a fairly regular basis. The counseling has, in most respects, gone well until recently. Due to changing life circumstances and a persistent unwillingness to take responsibility for those circumstances, M. was becoming more and more resistant in her sessions with my friend, looking for anyone to blame for the tangled circumstances of her life but herself. This would have been nothing more than a passing headache for my friend, but M. also possesses a strong talent for healing, a touch of sight, and a fair gift for magic, the latter of which she refuses to train.

When one has such a gift, an inborn psi-talent, and that gift is open and active, a responsible person has no choice but to train it. Why? The answer is quite simple: like unacknowledged emotions, an untrained gift has the potential to leak and to affect those in its general vicinity. Often untrained psi-gifts are tied into our emotions and when both emotions and gift are unexamined, unacknowledged, and unregulated, disaster can occur. This is what apparently has been occurring with M.

My friend told me that she had been hit with *malocchio*—the evil eye—by M. She was fairly irritated by the whole thing. Thankfully, being a competent magician, she had strong personal wards and her home was also well shielded. The taint did not penetrate the wards. What it did do was negatively affect anything outside of her house wards: namely lines of communication. That, combined with a warning from her ancestors and an oppressive darkness of mood that was not natural to her at that time, and a feeling of pressure on her shields from without, caused her to do divination to find the cause. She has practiced long enough to know when something is amiss. Her divination told her what spirit allies later confirmed: M. had put the evil eye on her. Oh, it surely wasn't intentional, but there was a great deal of insecurity, resentment and envy on M.'s part because my friend's life is going very, very well, especially financially. That was all it took. It was the second time this had happened. The first, occurring when my friend was in a vulnerable emotional state (and thus her shields weaker than usual) affected her with physical impairment (mirroring the same impairment in M.—M. had literally projected the mirror of her own injury onto my friend). After that, whenever she had to deal with M. she warded specifically against anything that might be leaking or inadvertently projected.

It gets even worse though. Upon scanning the threads of wyrd, doing further divination, and following a hunch later confirmed by one of her allies, my friend realized that M. had also thrown the eye onto a colleague who was causing her frustration at work, one toward whom she felt that same combination of resentment and envy. That is, after all, what really lies at the heart of the 'evil eye,' that particular combination of unacknowledged emotions. If one ever needed an esoteric example of why one should own one's shit, this is surely it.

This is what can happen when one doesn't self examine, when one doesn't take responsibility for oneself, when one is spiritually complacent and unwilling to admit to the existence of 'negative' emotions: leakage and harm. From what my friend told me, M. would never, ever admit to feeling any of these things because to do so would, in her own eyes, make her a bad person. It would also imply that she had to take responsibility for them. So instead of owning her issues, she'd apparently rather spew them onto every-one else for someone else to clean up. Let me just say that passive aggressiveness has no place in magic and no place in spiritual work *at all*.

For those wondering how to break the evil eye, I'll tell you what my friend did. She cleaned her house from top to bottom because physical clutter collects negative energy. She took a cleansing bath (dark beer, Florida water, some scented oil a beloved, recently deceased ancestor had given her, and alcohol that had been on the altar of her Patron Deity). She sprinkled Florida water all over the house. She called forth her allies to go and deal with the leakage, to send it back to its source or to devour it—whichever they preferred. She made offerings to all her ancestors and house spirits and asked for their protection. Then she checked over all her wards and worked a banishing charm on the remaining *ichor*. For a week, she wore protective charms, including one that contained a traditional Turkish charm against the evil eye: a blue glass bead with an eye worked into it. She also put the mother of all bindings on M. In all likelihood, she will have to further deal with this client in a way that neutralizes her ability to spew her own venom all over others. Fun times, my friends, fun times.

Sometimes people become toxic. This happens usually when they consistently refuse to take responsibility for themselves and their way of being in the world. Watch out for this. Toxicity is a contagion. There are numerous culturally specific methods to rid oneself of the evil eye, which is really just a blast of emotional toxicity that sticks. Some people have a talent for projecting that way, even though they often won't allow themselves to acknowledge it. I have found a regimen of cleansings combined with one or two banishing charms to be perfectly effective in removing such taint. Still, it is a bother. This really highlights the need for vigilance and consistency of practice. If one is doing regular energetic cleansings, grounding and centering properly, and maintaining consistent shields, it's fairly easy to recognize when something is amiss and to nip it in its proverbial bud.

This is why properly maintaining one's space is so very important. Ideally, one's dwelling should be so well maintained energetically that negative or malignant energies simply cannot find purchase. For years I dismissed the idea of the evil eye as mere superstition. I was wrong. When I was asked to write an introduction for this small book, I decided instead to send the above article. My own experiences with the evil eye made me look a second and third time at the traditional apotropaic charms, and to give far more credence to the tales of our grandparents and their grandparents than I ever would have when I was a novice magician just starting out in my studies. Now, familiarity with these charms is a foundational part of my work and I hope, after reading this book, it will become so for you as well. It's so simple to avoid *malocchio* and so easy to deal with if it's caught soon. The tools provided in this book are valuable tools to add to one's esoteric toolbox. I pray you, readers, take heed.

Sophie Reicher
Geneva, Switzerland
June 20, 2017

Chapter One

Thoughts about the evil eye range from Mesopotamian, Canaanite, Jewish, Syrian, and other Middle Eastern cultures, to Turkey and Greece, to Italy, up through Europe, and even into England (where you see it cropping up not only as the evil eye but in pre-Christian times as 'elf-shot'). Many scholars believe that it started in Sumer and spread outward from there. You don't much find it in South America, Asia, and Aboriginal cultures until the introduction of European influence. While today, the eye is associated largely with Islam, Judaism, and Mediterranean Christianity, awareness of the evil eye originated at least in ancient Sumer and here's where things get interesting.

You see, according to the ancient Sumerians, Babylonians, and Assyrians, the evil eye wasn't a thing, it was an evil *spirit*. It had sentience. This is where things get a little blurry (in part due to a paucity of sources). Many of the resulting charms against the evil eye are designed to 'frighten it away,' 'reflect back the gaze,' or, in some cases, 'to cause amusement and thus avert malevolent intent' of some unseen force. At the same time, especially in later and even contemporary sources, the evil eye is addressed as something that can be thrown upon a victim by someone else. My own theory is that it is both: that there is a malignant spirit (something analogous to the Osogbo of Lukumi, spirits of various types of ills and misfortunes) that can plague a person, *when its attention is attracted* by the malevolently focused gaze of someone with a particular ability, the skill of casting the evil eye. I believe it is the energetic tag or taint, the miasma created or summoned forth by that malignant gaze and the emotions behind it that paves the way for the evil eye to harass and strike.

I'd like to tell you about one of my own brushes with *malocchio* (Italian for 'evil eye'). I've actually been hit with it twice. I offer these situations up because they will hopefully give you some idea of how this can work. An awful lot of the folklore on the evil eye focuses on its effect on children, something we'll talk about below, but you don't read too much about how it can affect adults.

The first time I was struck, I knew very little about *malocchio*, and I responded like a conjure woman (and the only reason I think I recognized it for what it was, lay in the sheer obviousness of the symptoms' cause and effect). I've become more nuanced in my treatment of it over the years, but I still stand by my initial response to it as something potentially life threatening, dangerous, and demanding clear and immediate response.

The woman who inadvertently cast it onto me, came to visit with an inflamed left eye and right ankle. She had a baseball size swelling on her Achilles tendon (both of us are ex-ballet dancers and had tendonitis). I sat opposite her and by the time she left, I had an inflamed right eye, and a baseball size swelling on my left ankle and my ancestors were livid. I did a series of cleansings and attended to it as best I knew how and fortunately in this case, given that I caught it immediately, this was enough to rid me of the taint. I talked about this with a friend of mine and began to hash out my own theories of how this all works.

The second time was a bit more insidious and took me about two weeks to realize what was happening. It started with small things going wrong… nothing noticeable, until it progressed to accidents including glassware flying off the shelf onto my head, a random choking incident that nearly involved three firemen giving me the Heimlich in a restaurant bathroom and five or six other close calls (to danger or death) *in the same day*. My husband finally insisted we sit down and divine because it was getting too obvious to ignore. After that, we did a series of cleansings and I had a friend, a conjure man, also cleanse me. That finally removed the taint and I wore apotropaic charms for the next three months every single day.

There were distinct similarities in the nature of the women who threw this onto me:[*] they were all very jealous and envious of my circumstances, in one case because I was financially stable and in the other because I had a loving and stable relationship, they were also passive aggressive— unable or unwilling to admit and claim their anger let alone express it. Both had been strongly conditioned to see the expression of anger as morally wrong. Instead, they held it inside and let it simmer, salting it with a liberal dose of envy and ill intent. Both were also above average in psi-talent (but refused training) and this combination provided a hothouse in which the ability to cast a potentially lethal taint was born.

Those are really the keys to the evil eye: envy, jealousy and malice. I'll tell you something else that may likely blow your mind (but anthropological/folkloric literature also confirms it): most people who throw the evil eye *don't know they're doing it*. Moreover, many would be horrified to realize they were causing harm. Throughout the accounts I've read, my own experiences, and conversations with colleagues, these traits are the common denominator. You'll

---

[*] I, by the way, lack the ability to throw the evil eye. I rather think to throw the eye one must of necessity be passive aggressive, and that's one thing of which I've never been accused!

see this hinted at in many folkloric accounts which inevitably focus on children: a child gets hit with the evil eye when envy is aroused by praise. So, in many cultures, children are not praised and if a child does receive praise, the mother or another relative may perform certain warding gestures. In one account that I the folklorist noted that he was almost exposed to actual violence because he'd complimented the host's children so. He felt pressured into performing a ritual (spitting on the child) to symbolically revoke and reverse his praise, praise that might attract the attention of evil spirits.

Catherine Yronwode, of luckymojo.com, notes that "Only in Sicily and Southern Italy is it believed that some people can DELIBERATELY cast the evil eye on others. There the regionally idiosyncratic belief is that certain people (including at least one former Pope) are born with the evil eye and 'project' it involuntarily. Such people are called *jettatores* ('projectors') and their specific form of evil eye is called *jettatura* ('projection') in contradistinction to the garden variety of envious or praising evil eye, which in Italian is called *mal occhio* ('bad eye'). *Jettatores* are not necessarily evil or envious people, according to this belief system, and they are often represented as being saddened and embarrassed by the harm they cause."

Many scholars (like Alan Dundes) believe that at its root, the evil eye is a process of 'drying up,' citing the origins of the evil eye in desert cultures where water would have been a premium. This is not inaccurate. What it causes is a drying up of one's luck and how that manifests depends on where the weaknesses in one's wyrd (the fabric of one's luck/life/destiny/choices) may be. Early Akkadian sources refer to the Evil Eye's approach as causing drought and the rotting of food (see the article on Mesopotamian sources by Thomsen cited at the end of this chapter). It also causes chaos in one's life, if the necessary fault lines exist wherein this can gain

9

purchase. None of us are perfect—there are always fault lines!

Some of the noticeable symptoms include:

- ❖ sudden memory issues
- ❖ headaches
- ❖ general and unspecified malaise and ill health
- ❖ repeated loss of opportunities
- ❖ sudden recurrent vexations
- ❖ unspecified anxiety, accidents—particularly when they occur in sudden clusters
- ❖ arguments—for no apparent reason
- ❖ generic and ongoing aggravations—particularly when they start suddenly and accompany any of these other symptoms
- ❖ sudden bad luck

Vague? Yes, and you have to look at the pattern and look for the taint. If you can sense/see wyrd, it can sometimes be spotted there. If you have the Sight, it is obvious, though can be sneaky. Obviously, *rule out any medical conditions*! Look at the circumstances: when did this start? Is the person a general mess, or are their lives more or less in order? Sometimes, if you ask if they've anyone in their lives who is particularly envious, the client will have an immediate sense of who is responsible. I would always confirm via divination. Sometimes you can actually track the cause and effect.

The two traditional ways that I learned to diagnose it are Eastern European and Mediterranean respectively (I've also seen this second technique come up in Middle Eastern practice occasionally):

1. After praying (I pray to my ancestors), drop burnt match heads (I was told nine) in a pan of water. If

they float, the evil eye is present.

2. Again, after praying, drip nine drops of olive oil into a basin of water, one drop at a time. If, within the first minute, the drops come together to form a blob (particularly if it's 'eye' shaped), the evil eye is present. Do not wait—after a few minutes, it's going to run together naturally!

I've also read about a technique where you drip melted wax into holy water, and if it splatters the side of the bowl, or sticks to the side of the bowl, the evil eye is present. I've never used this technique though. There are other techniques as well, but these two are the ones that I find relatively reliable (I usually use the olive oil).

Even if I do this, I prefer to verify via divination. I'll often use a pendulum or Hermes' coins. This latter is a very simple system of divination you can use. It's sacred to Hermes, who is a God of luck, chance, travel, communication, gambling, thievery, and many other things. My husband Sannion contributed this part of the chapter, since he has had a longer devotion to Hermes than I. Hermes is pretty easy-going, at least I've found Him so with this particular process, but I would still make an offering to Him before using it.

SANNION'S LESSON

Hermes was connected with all sorts of humble forms of divination in antiquity. According to the 4th *Homeric Hymn* Apollo would not grant his brother a share of Delphi's famed oracular prophecy, but instead gave him the bee-maidens "who know how to speak the truth" to divine with, and Zeus commanded that "glorious Hermes should be lord over all birds of omen and grim-eyed lions, and boars with gleaming tusks, and over dogs and all flocks that the wide earth nourishes" (568a-573) whose movements could predict the future if men were inclined to learn the art of interpretation from him. Hermes was also sought to grant prophetic dreams (Odyssey 7.137), presided over divination by knuckle-bones, dice, or pebbles (Apollodoros 3.115) and *kledones* or omens derived from overheard conversations (Pausanias 7.22.2).

In keeping with this spirit, modern Hellenic polytheists have come up with a very simple form of divination which is especially appropriate for Hermes since he is also the god of commerce and the inventor of money (Suidas s.v. Hermes). While it is fairly primitive and can't expound on the complexities of a given situation, it can be quite helpful in a pinch, especially when you need decisive answers. And when used properly you can actually manage to tease out a good deal of information from it.

Basically, the system works like this. First you should pray to Hermes in your customary manner and ask him to grant you insight on the given issue. You may either choose to speak your question aloud or do so silently, as I haven't noticed a difference one way or the other. Then take out three coins. Ideally they should all be of the same value, so that each factor is given equal importance, but if you only have mixed coins in your pocket that will do. Three coins is best, that way your answer won't come out a stalemate as might happen with four, an otherwise preferred Hermetic number, and you will also have enough information to consider the question properly. Using only one coin limits the effectiveness of the oracle, although in a pinch that works too.

Toss the coins and note how they land.

❖ Three heads indicates a definitive YES.

❖ Three tails indicates a definitive NO.

❖ Two heads and one tail indicates a generally favorable outcome, though there may be some minor conflict involved; there may also be some contingency you're not aware of and should look into more; or consent is only grudgingly offered, and while it will likely come about, it perhaps should not.

❖ Two tails and one head indicates a generally un-favorable outcome, one which has a chance of being salvaged though it will require a great deal of effort to do so; too little is known about a situation to provide a definitive answer; you should examine your motives and see why you're still clinging to this hope even when you know that it won't be.

There are other ways that you can interpret the fall of coins, especially in the context of your question, and as with most forms of divination you should allow your intuition to guide you.

This form can be very useful when you are trying to gain a diagnostic understanding of things. One question can lead into others as you pare down all of the probabilities. However, as with all forms of divination once you have received a clear answer you should stop asking, as to continue is considered very bad form and potentially insulting to the divinity.

It is also important to understand when to consult the oracle. It's okay to use it when faced with a situation where you cannot possibly determine which of two options is the best, or when you are trying to ascertain information you have no other way of obtaining, or you need a quick goad to spur your thoughts into motion. However, when you already know what the outcome is going to be, or you are using it as a crutch so that you don't ever have to make a decision for yourself - then you have a problem. It is also important to understand that the information you receive holds true only for yourself. If you want to know what another person is thinking just come out and ask them! Don't try to weasel your way into their thoughts or hold them accountable for what comes out during the oracle. If you do that Hermes just might lead you astray in order to prove a point.

Although you can use any change in your pocket for this —especially if you're on the fly and in need of quick assistance—I've found that reserving three coins for special use as your divinatory tool can be very effective, especially if these coins are of foreign extraction, since Hermes is the god of travelers. If you use such a miscellany of coins it's okay if they don't all have the same face value, provided they do have both a discernible head and tail.

After you have finished your consultation you should thank Hermes for his guidance, and abide by what comes out. If you continuously disregard his advice he will eventually stop offering it.

I have to say, though, regardless of how the divination comes out, I strongly advocate regular cleansings. I'm all about prevention, prevention, prevention. Also, regardless of what any of the traditional diagnostic methods show, *always* confirm with divination and trust your gut. (I also tend to think that reading about it can carry with it some level of minor danger—of attracting its attention—so always do a cleansing afterwards too and perhaps even wear evil eye charms whilst reading. I tend to do this anyway as a matter of course).

I want to close by noting that I do *not* consider the evil eye to be any type of curse. In most cases, it's an inadvertent side effect of envy and malice.

SUGGESTED READING

Lykiardopoulos, Amica. "The Evil Eye: Towards an Exhaustive
   Study." *Folklore* 92:2 (1981): 221-230.
Murgoci, A. "The Evil Eye in Roumania, and Its Antidotes."
   Folklore 34:4 (1923): 357-362.
Thomsen, Marie-Louise. "The Evil Eye in Mesopotamia."
   Journal of Near Eastern Studies 51:1 (1992): 19-32.

Chapter Two

efore we delve further into the evil eye, I want to give you a few really good exercises that will help you develop your sensitivity to spirits, energy, the Holy Powers, et al. It will really help in this type of work and will even help develop any latent sensitivities you may have. They're useful for staying clean and doing this work mindfully. The exercises are, I will grant you, a little boring (at least I find them so) but they lead to overall psychic, emotional, and spiritual health when done regularly. You can even use them in your regular work day to cope with stress. I've taught them to business men and women for just that reason.

My friend Sophie Reicher has written an excellent little book called *Spiritual Protection*, where she gives a lot of these exercises too and I highly recommend it. I'm going to jump right into the exercises first. They're not at all difficult, I promise you, but they teach the mind to focus, to hit the appropriate meditative state where really good and productive discernment can occur. I recommend doing them for a minimum of ten minutes a day. That's not too much (set a kitchen timer or stop watch if you want) and you will see results.

The first and most important exercises that one can do are grounding and centering. These two simple exercises are the backbone of any spiritual or esoteric practice. They are also, as noted above, extraordinarily useful for dealing with stress and tension. I've also found that they can be an effective tool in managing a bad temper! I learned how to center in a martial arts class, via a breathing exercise called the Four-Fold Breath, which I shall present here. This is not a difficult exercise. All it takes is time. The breath pattern itself will center you. Centering is a multi-faceted process: it gives you breathing room to effectively act rather than react to what's happening around you; it pinpoints your actual, physical center; it helps you establish a personal boundary, to determine where you end and the outside world begins; it aligns the energetic and physical bodies so that both occupy the same space; and it helps one to cope with and effective process random emotions and energies to which one might be exposed throughout the day or the work.

To do this breathing exercise, simply inhale four counts, hold four counts, exhale four counts, hold four counts. Do this over and over for about ten minutes. You can do this anywhere. You have to breathe, after all!

I recommend practicing this several times a day. The good thing about this exercise is that you can do it while going about your daily business and no one need be the wiser. I like to give myself a mnemonic to remind myself to practice. For instance, you might say "every time I see a silver car, I am going to center, ground, and check my personal shields." That would not be too frequent, by the way. The key is consistency and regularity of practice.

In time, as you breathe, you want to feel all the breath, all the random energies in your body gathering about three inches below the naval. Eventually, as you breathe, you want to feel the energy gathering in a glowing golden ball at this point. A student of mine once put it this way: "Basically, centering is 'contemplating your naval!'" She was right too. Be sure to breathe through your diaphragm taking deep, even breaths. Don't rush and don't worry if your mind wanders. Just gently bring it back to the breath. One caveat: large busted women and most men center higher, at the solar plexus and even sometimes in the heart chakra area. There is nothing esoteric about this; it's pure body mechanics and physiology. Find your physical center and that's where your esoteric center should also be. One's center is based on where one's center of gravity is. As I noted above, for most women, that is in the hips, the second chakra area. Some larger, or large busted women, and most men center at the solar plexus or in some cases even higher. Centering creates a necessary boundary: it demarcates where you begin and end and where the outside world begins and ends.

Now, once you're centered and once the energy in your body has been collected, it has to go somewhere. Grounding adds stability, it gives one a connection to the earth; it makes one strong, flexible, and resilient. Basically grounding is just sending all the energy/tension/emotions that have been collected in the body, down into the earth. (Science tells us that everything is energy in motion, which means tension, stress, and emotions are energy too and energy can be worked with.) Don't worry if you can't see or feel anything….start with the mental focus and eventually your awareness of the internal flow of energy will increase.

The easiest grounding exercise to begin with is also, like centering, a breathing exercise. Inhale and feel the energy gathered in your center. Now, as you exhale, feel that energy exiting the body through the root chakra (the perianal area) or through the feet, though I find the root chakra is the more stable point. Some practices place the root right at the end of the tail bone—which is interesting after you've spent thirty years working it at the perineum. Try both and see which one works best for you. There are pros and cons to teach method. Anyway, as you breathe, on the second exhale, feel it entering the earth and branching out into a thick, sturdy network of roots. Continue this

18

imagery for as long as you need to, using each ensuing exhalation to take you further and further into the earth until you feel fully grounded. You can use this visualization and breathing technique to rid your body of tension, stress, even physical pain. I've used it to unknot spasming muscles, imagining that I was inhaling and exhaling through the knot itself.

Now, in time you will want to learn different ways of grounding, and you will find that many of the exercises are primarily visualization exercises. Now, don't worry if you're not good at visualizing things....that too is a skill that comes in time. I always had difficulty with it. You may find that the image comes via feelings instead of sight and that's okay too. Just like people have different learning styles, some being visual, some auditory, some more kinesthetic in various combinations, the same holds true for meditation and energy work. Don't sweat it, just start where you start.

Some people find it helpful to send energy down through the feet as they walk. That is a useful secondary grounding technique. The idea is that you're connecting yourself to something bigger than you are, and that something (the earth beneath your feet) can support and sustain you. It gives you a focal point upon which you are an axis. The standard idea with grounding is to be a tree. Once you've gathered the energy at your naval, send it down through the root chakra visualizing a tap root and rich network of smaller roots reaching deep into the earth. The root chakra is where one connects to the earth, to primal life energy. Send all the energy down, timing it to each exhalation, into the earth. See it streaming from your root chakra in a solid golden cord of energy. This cord goes down through the floor, through the foundations of the house and into the earth, it reaches very deeply and with each ex-halation see it branching off like roots of a tree, tying you tightly to the earth.

These two exercises are pre-requisites to being able to shield effectively. The only requirement to gaining excellence is practice. As my Russian teacher told me when I was in high school: repetition is the mother of learning. That holds especially true here.

Some people balk at the idea of 'shielding.' It sounds harsh and divisive. In reality shielding is just about maintaining good boundaries and you need too personal boundaries to be a healthy human being and to maintain healthy relationships. A shield is a filter, one that you control, that helps in filtering out what is not you, all the stimuli that we face on a day to day basis. For people with strong psychic gifts it's a necessity and for people with lighter talents it's also a good and useful tool to have in one's metaphysical toolbox.

If you're poo-pooing the idea of energy work, then think of this as a mental exercise: visualize or imagine or feel a transparent wall, like plexiglass between yourself and others... try this in your job when a toxic co-worker or client (we all have them) is harassing you: nothing they put off can penetrate. See if it makes a difference in how you come away from those stressful encounters.

Shielding is all about developing strong, flexible boundaries. I find that the people who have trouble maintaining good boundaries in other areas of their lives usually suck at shielding. They're also the ones who could benefit the most from it and who resist it the most fervently. I once actually had a client say to me: "I don't want to learn to shield. I want to be one with the universe." I'm afraid I was tired, aggravated, and a bit more blunt than I probably should have been: "Yeah, sweetheart. The universe is going to crush you like an empty beer can. Sit the f*ck down and shield." But that's me: spreading diplomacy everywhere I go.

Perhaps it's best to think of a shield as a boundary or filter that you can strengthen or lighten or take down completely depending on the situation. One of the reasons it's so helpful is that it allows you to pinpoint what's you, what's an ancestor, what's Deity, what's white noise from the chaos in the minds around you, etc. It's also good, as I noted above, for stress. So how do you do it? Well, just as you send energy down through your ground, you can pull it up again. I would suggest centering, grounding and then pulling energy up on the inhalation and feeling it rise up around you fully encasing you. This is the most basic shield. Then you can tweak it to your own specifications. I do not recommend the New Age 'white light' shield for the sole reasons that (a) it's not very effective; and (b) it's very noticeable. Reicher gives quite a few different shielding techniques in her book and I recommend experimenting. You can even ask your ancestors for help.

While shielding is something of an advanced technique (I recommend focusing on centering and grounding for a few weeks first), one thing that everyone should do often and consistently is cleansing. It's very important when doing spiritual work to keep yourself spiritually and energetically clean. This is one of the ways that we can heighten our spiritual receptivity and what spirit workers call 'signal clarity': the ability to receive (in whatever way it happens) and correctly recognize and interpret information, communication, and messages from the Gods, ancestors, and spirits.

There are dozens and dozens of ways to cleanse. The most common is probably a cleansing bath. (If you don't have a bathtub, don't worry. The really traditional way of doing a cleansing bath is to pour the mixture over your head. It's much more comfortable though to add stuff to a hot bath!) Here are a few of my favorites:

1. Add a can of dark beer to your bath. It totally cleanses the energetic body. (German folk custom)
2. One cup of apple cider vinegar, one cup of sea salt.
3. One cup of Florida water.
4. A cup of pink salt, or if you're really gunked up, black salt.

You can also make up various combinations of herbs and add a little rum and call it a day. I recommend Cat Yronwode's book *Hoodoo Herb and Root Magic* because it gives appendices that list the spiritual usage of many different herbs and it's easy to mix and match. Usually the formula for most spiritual baths calls for three different ingredients and then a cologne like Florida water, or rum, or ammonia or something like that. Play around and see what works best. I like cinnamon, frankincense, allspice, a bit of orange water and a dash of rum as a good blessing bath. All those herbs are associated with good fortune and wealth and spiritual abundance.

But really, pour some beer in your bath and call it a day if this is troubling to you. I would also suggest showering and changing your clothes as soon as you come in from work. We pick up an awful lot of psychic and energetic gunk in our work day. It's best to be clean from it as soon as possible. There are dozens and dozens of ways to cleanse energetically. One thing that I've actually employed that sounds a little strange (yes, stranger than a beer bath!) is very useful if you know you've really collected a lot of psychic or energetic pollution, or you feel a spirit is tracking you, but you can't change clothes: turn them inside out. It's an old remedy for when you're traveling and being harassed by the fae. It breaks the energetic connection temporarily. I'd still change clothes and bathe as soon as I could, though, afterwards.

Those are the four basic exercises that I feel are

fundamental to clean spiritual work. Most importantly, as you become more aware and mindful, you're more likely to recognize when something is amiss around you and more likely to pay heed to what you're sensing, all very important when dealing with the evil eye.

SUGGESTED READING

Clarke, Mary Washington. "Evil Eye in Southern Italy." *Western Folklore* 23:2 (1964): 123-124.
Gubbins, J. K. "Some Observations on the Evil Eye in Modern Greece." *Folklore* 57:4 (1946): 195-198.
Wazana, Nili. "A Case of the Evil Eye: Qohelet 4:4-8." *Journal of Biblical Literature* 126:4 (2007): 685-702.

Chapter Three

It's important to keep doing the basic exercises in Chapter Two on an ongoing basis because over time, they really do help bolster one's clear psychic sensitivity and spiritual discernment. At the very least, you'll become more aware of when something is out of balance and amiss and that's important for this type of work. The Evil Eye is all about creating an imbalance.

Many sources, as you will encounter in the readings I've suggested thus far, talk about the eye as a type of 'drying up.' it might be drying up of health, milk, abundance, or luck, but the result is a precarious brittleness, a lack of the energetic lubrication that allows us to move well and relatively unscathed through an average day.

No one ever thinks of the evil eye! It's not the only type of malignancy that can be targeted on a person and it's not a curse. I reserve that latter term specifically for a conjuration that is worked with intent and focus and deep desire to harm. In most cases, as I noted in Chapter One, the person casting the evil eye isn't doing it consciously. If they could actually own their anger and envy and hostility in an adult way, after all, they wouldn't be *able* to cast the eye! (I've never had much patience with passive aggressive behavior, less so since encountering the eye a couple of times.) So before we delve into what to do once you know a person has been hit, I want to talk about ways to recognize when someone has been hit and then we'll go into how to treat it.

Firstly, after diagnosing this (and I'll get to the how of

that in a moment), I always, always, always confirm via divination. If you find that you have absolutely no skill as a diviner (and it is a specific talent; you may not be able to do it beyond the most rudimentary of binary systems and that's okay), then your next step would be to cultivate a working relationship with a couple of solid diviners whom you can call to verify and double check. This is one of the purposes of divination: to keep things flowing smoothly spiritually and in your everyday life, and to identify and head off problems. It's a sacred art and there was a time in our ancestral past when armies would not move until the oracles or diviners gave the okay. There's a lovely quote that I keep in my office by Sarah Iles Johnson that says that "divination more than any other religious act, confirms not only that the gods exist, but that they pay attention to us." We no longer treat it as such and in part there is both two thousand years of monotheistic oppression and the Protestant reformation to thank. It's become at best a parlor trick, but for those of us restoring our ancient polytheisms, picking up those threads and bringing our traditions back, divination is a very, very sacred thing, not to be taken lightly. The important thing is that you in some way confirm your 'diagnosis.'

I have found that the most common symptoms of the Eye are ongoing accidents—too many to be coincidence, malaise (quite often the flow of vital energy in the body has been mucked with), and 'bad luck,' maybe even general confusion. There may be other symptoms too that overlap with what I would consider the symptoms of a curse or psychic attack (headache, unspecified feeling bad, dizziness, paranoia, dread, etc.). If there are any physical symptoms, even if you are 100% sure that it's the Eye, it's best to always suggest strongly that the person see a doctor for a full check up. CYA, folks. (Also even if it's caused by the Eye or a curse, the physical ailments are real and can trigger a host of other complaints that may not go away without medical help. Always err on the side of caution.)

You'll also want to keep an eye out—no pun intended—for those with emotional problems that may lead them to seek attention by creating drama in their lives. When I initially gave this material as an online course I was teaching spirit workers, and in that line of work you'll encounter your fair share of people with emotional problems, trust me. The thing is, that they may be self-absorbed, insecure, drama-seeking, or emotionally and/or mentally ill doesn't render them immune to the Eye. Use your best judgment but do not allow yourself to be pulled into the ongoing saga of their drama. Just don't. It's not your job and it's going to pull you away from the sacred work that you yourself have to do (and we each have something for which we were put on this earth). You can't fix them. If I sound harsh here, consider that I have been teaching and serving as a priest since 1995, working in part with a community that almost seems to encourage such things. My work is important to me. Serving the Gods and ancestors well is important to me. Getting entangled with folks like this beyond the most cursory of professional capacities (and sometimes even then) furthers neither. It will lead to frustration, miasma, and burnout.

For those of you who are psychically gifted, you may sense or even see the mark of the Eye on someone. I can sense it, but I've been told by those with the Sight that it almost looks like a caul has been put over the person. Pay attention to your gut when you have folks coming to you who have been having 'accidents.' I would, in consultation, pray and then divine, and I might use a binary system like the Hermes coin divination from Chapter One to confirm. If you have the skill, do a full reading for them. Then, you may also follow up with one of the diagnostic tools we have already discussed. I would not rely on just one thing. If you're getting inconclusive results, treat it as the Eye. This type of evil spirit/contagion is tricky. It will hide and attempt to prolong its influence. The energetic tag itself is sometimes difficult to scope out because it can be lost under the avalanche of bad luck that has begun to befall the client. So when in doubt, act as if.

Once I'd diagnosed the Eye (or once I'd decided the case was ambiguous enough that I'm going to go on the assumption that the Eye is present—after all, cleansing a person isn't going to hurt them so you won't be doing harm even if you're wrong—I'll proceed in the following way:

If I'm a good diviner, I'll do a full read to try to suss out where the Eye came from and any other pertinent information I should know. Sometimes when you mention the evil eye, the person will just have an instinctive response: they'll know where it came from. If I weren't a diviner, I'd either call a colleague for a consult via phone or Skype on the spot, or have the client schedule later for follow up with a diviner. (As an aside, when I divine, I have an evil eye charm laying on the divination mat between me and my client, and I'm likely wearing one as well as a matter of course.)

As an aside, one of the traditional beliefs concerning the Eye is that praise and flattery are potentially harmful. I was reminded of this recently when a Lebanese friend was visiting. I had complimented her sweater, which was gorgeous and something she'd made herself. She instinctively and automatically began pointing out all the flaws. Later she told me that she realized it was a culturally ingrained thing: she was instinctively trying to ward off the evil eye, which can be attracted by such praise (which is why in many cultures you never praise children). In fact, when I was initially researching for this course, I found an anthropological account in which a man said he almost came to violence when he was doing his field work. He was in a

Mediterranean country (I don't recall which), and had been visiting acquaintances. They had a beautiful child and he made one too many compliments. They forced him nearly at threat of violence to perform an apotropaic ritual to ward off the eye from the child. There are many such rituals, a frightening number of which involve spitting. Anyway, the crux of this is that excessive flattery, or in some cases any flattery at all can be viewed as an attempt to cast or attract the Eye).

So, after I'd divined, I'd employ one of the methods for diagnosing the Eye—probably the olive oil one or Sannion's technique (given below). Then I'd get down to business:[†]

A. If you are able to pinpoint from where the Eye originates, any items received from that person need to be thrown away or burned.

B. I would go through a series of cleansings: If I felt I had the skill (it usually takes healing hands), I might anoint my hands with a blessing oil and rub the person down from head to toe with the intent to tear away the mark of the eye. If I didn't feel confident in this (and I personally don't—I don't have that gift), I would mix up a combination of 3 parts rue (an herb known for its power against the evil eye), 1 part mugwort, 1 part cedar, 1/2 part tobacco, 1/2 part sage (maybe a little copal crushed and added so it burns better) and light this over self-starting charcoal (small charcoals you can find in any occult, esoteric or New Age store). Get a good smoke going and completely immerse the person. Carry your incense burner with the charcoal and herbs around the person, outlining their aura. Have them stand over it too.

[†] It doesn't hurt to do divination to choose the best method of removing the Eye.

Pray as you do this to the Gods and ancestors (whichever of the Holy Powers you venerate the most) to remove the Eye and cleanse this person restoring harmony and balance, restoring proper flow.

C. Then I would have them (on the spot) take a cleansing bath. To the bath add *one* of the following:

1. a very strong infusion of rue (if the person is pregnant do not use rue)
2. a can of dark beer
3. blessed salt, Florida water, holy water (if you're ordained, make your own), apple cider vinegar, rum, and sometimes to that, to draw *good* things, I add citrus, cinnamon, and sugar (sometimes I have them take a second bath later with this)

Make sure the person is instructed to completely submerge themselves. *The use of fluids counteracts and balances out the dryness caused by the Eye itself.*[‡]

D. Some people will take a fresh egg (and it's best if it can be a fertilized one) and rub it all over the person's body while praying fervently (traditional root workers will say the Lord's prayer or Psalm 23; polytheists use a prayer to the Deity or Deities of their choice or ancestors). Then that egg is taken outside to a crossroads and dashed either against the ground or against a tree. I would still follow up with a cleansing bath though.

[‡‡] While fire is an excellent means of cleansing most things, I would not recommend its use with the Eye....the Eye needs to be countered by the introduction of liquid and flow.

E. If you have a blessed and consecrated blade, you can crush rue and burn it as incense, run the blade through the smoke, and with prayers, scrape around the person's aura, energetically cutting away any taint (do not really cut the person!). But you have to (a) have a sacred blade; and (b) carry a measure of warrior medicine for this to work.

F. Finally, after the cleansing bath, I would anoint the client with either Blessing oil or more preferably Fiery Wall of Protection oil afterwards and recommend they carry apotropaic charms for the next three months, daily. I'd also tell them to thoroughly clean their homes of clutter. I've included some traditional recipes for each oil at the end of this chapter.

One note of caution: you need to protect yourself when you're doing this type of work, particularly if you're regularly seeing clients. I recommend regular cleansing baths and I always either wear, or have on the divination mat between me and my clients, an evil eye charm. I suspect, though I have no proof, that the Eye can transfer from client to spirit worker, or that it is contagious. Avoid touching them without protections. Be very careful and take precautions.

SANNION'S EVIL EYE CURE[§]

The grace of Elais, Spermo and Oino

"Liber gave my girls gifts greater than their pious prayers. For at my daughters' touch all things were turned to corn or wine or

---

[§] Excerpted with permission from *Hunting Wisdom: A Bacchic Orphic Diviner's Manual* by H. Jeremiah Lewis, aka Sannion.

oil of Minerva's tree. Rich was that role of theirs!" (Ovid, *Metamorphoses* 13. 631)

A drop of olive oil is placed in a glass of *chernips*. If the drop floats you are fine, but if it sinks then it means you have the evil eye on you.

Another method: place two drops of olive oil in the *chernips*; if the drops stay separated, there is no cause for worry. If they cohere, move on to the next stage: Take a handful of barley groats and say the following while scattering them across your doorstep:

"You, baneful one, cannot afflict me until you have counted every last one of these grains! And if you should try, well, I know a spell of Orpheus, a most excellent one, to make the brand enter your skull of its own accord, and set alight the one-eyed son of Earth! What ho! my gallants, thrust away, make haste and burn his eyebrow off, the monster's a guest-devouring foe. Oh! singe and scorch the shepherd of Aetna; twirl the brand and drag it round and be careful lest in his agony he treat thee to some wantonness."

Then wash your hands and face in wine over which the following words (from the *Orations* of Aelius Aristides) have been spoken:

"Nothing can be so firmly bound by illness, by wrath or by fortune   that cannot be released by the Lord Dionysos."

SUGGESTED READING

Italian-American Tales. "The Maloik (Malochhio) or the 'Evil Eye.'" Posted January 16, 2009. http://sigime. blogspot.com/2009/01/maloik-malocchio.html.

Lele, Ócha'ni. *Osogbo: Speaking to the Spirits of Misfortune.* Destiny Books, 2014.

Lewis, H. Jeremiah. *Hunting Wisdom: A Bacchic Orphic Diviner's Manual.* Nysa Press, 2016.

A FEW USEFUL RECIPES

Fiery Wall of Protection Oil

- frankincense
- a pinch of cayenne pepper
- rue
- few drops of sandalwood essential oil
- pinch of angelica
- a few drops of cinnamon essential oil (Be careful with this. I usually prefer to add a cinnamon stick to the bottle. Cinnamon oil can give you a nasty burn.)
- pinch of salt (bless it first)
- few drops of ginger essential oil or a peeled piece of ginger
- 1-3 bay leaves
- chunk of dragonsblood resin
- few drops of black pepper essential oil or nine peppercorns

Add the above ingredients to a bottle of either pure olive oil or sweet almond oil. I prefer the latter.

Blessing oil[**]

- frankincense

[**] This is a variation on Cat Yronwode's blessing oil, which is itself a variation on a traditional conjure recipe.

- benzoin, finely ground
- few drops essential oil of frankincense
- few drops essential oil of benzoin
- one of the following rose scents (I like Rose Otto but real rose fragrance is terribly expensive. synthetics are okay here.):
  - essential oil of roses (Rose Otto)
  - essential oil of rose geranium
  - rose fragrance (synthetic)
  - rose petals

Top with carrier oil, preferably almond oil with vitamin E (e.g., almond oil which has been dosed with Vitamin E).

My blessing oil

- frankincense
- myrrh
- copal
- few drops of sandalwood oil
- few drops of benzoin oil
- small piece of dragonsblood
- sweet almond oil with a bit of vitamin E

You can turn these into incenses by using the herb instead of essential oils.

Chapter Four

An ounce of prevention really is worth a pound of cure, and this is especially true with the Evil Eye. In this chapter, I'm going to be discussing apotropaic charms—charms to ward off evil, in this case, the evil eye. I used to poo-poo all the traditional charms, especially the often gaudy blue glass 'eye' beads, but I found out the hard way that there's something to them! So I'm going to go over those and other similar and popular ways to protect oneself.

Firstly, the idea with many charms is to either (a) gaze back at the eye, blocking its power; or (b) to cause it sudden, unexpected amusement and thus turn the creature's (remember in the oldest texts it's an evil spirit) wrath away. Remember also that envy, jealousy, and anger are often the sources of the eye (or if we look at it as an evil spirit, that which causes the psychic mark/intent that calls it). Many of the charms are behavioral modification pieces designed to avoid calling attention to one's boons, benefits, and blessings.

This latter category is particularly something one sees with children, though as I noted earlier, I recently ran into it with an adult colleague as well. This is the reason why you will not often hear exceptional children praised in certain areas—why, if a child is praised, the parent or guardian will spit three times to the side, or will immediately counter by mentioning the child's failings. Sometimes you'll hear the exact opposite of a complement—"Oh, she's an ugly little thing"—but said in an affectionate way. It's all to avoid drawing envy, eliciting jealousy, and thus catching the attention of the Eye. This can be taken so far as to refuse outright any praise given to a child, spitting on the child to counter the potentially malignant praise, or in some cases dressing the child in an ugly way or putting soot or dirt on the child. I've never seen this last in practice, but I have encountered the first two quite a bit.

In Italy you may see a protective hand gesture used when someone feels they are potentially being threatened with the eye: the middle two fingers will be folded down so that the little finger, first finger and thumb make 'horns' (this is the *mano cornuto*—the horned hand). It's esoterically a means of meeting 'like with like' and thus canceling out the harm. There's also the *mano fico*, the fig hand, where a fist is made and the thumb is pushed through the first and second finger. The idea is the same: to banish the evil eye. Sometimes you can find charms of a 'hand of power' in each of these configurations, as well, that can be worn.

The Udjat eye or eye of Horus was designed to ward off the evil eye and I've known people to wear the ankh for this purpose as well. Certain stones like agate or black tourmaline, or shells like a cat's eye shell or most notably and common a cowrie, are also said to have apotropaic potential.

The two most common (and what I personally prefer to use) are the kappa hand—also called the hand of Fatima or hamsa hand (which symbolizes the Canaanite God Ilu's hand of protection guarding the heart and warding away all harm)—and the blue eye beads. You've all seen those things right? They're blue beads that have a stylized eye. Sometimes you can even find eyeball beads, beads that are shaped like an eye and look disturbingly like the real thing too. I usually wear bracelets of the blue eye beads, or a hamsa necklace. I cleanse these regularly in the smoke of rue or by using Florida water.

The color, by the way, may be significant. Blue is the rarest color in nature. In many cultures it was considered extremely holy because it was the color of 'heaven.' I've seen eye beads in other colors but I've never found them to be quite as effective (I'll wear them but combined with the more traditional blue beads). Sometimes you can find hamsa hand pendants with the blue eye bead inset. Coral and turquoise are also protective.

In some areas, like India, mirrors are worn or carried to reflect the Eye back. I tend not to recommend this solely because I find mirrors can make the energy around one jagged, but this is sound esoteric practice. You see it with Mongolian shamans as well with their reflective shield charms (called *toli*).

Sometimes red thread will be tied around a baby's wrist for protection. I've known adults to wear it as well. I believe this hearkens back to the Neolithic era when red ochre was one of the most sacred substances and used as a blood substitute in rituals. It may also tie into Egyptian protective charms, representing the blood of Isis.

The Italian horn-shaped amulets which represent the phallus or quite honestly, charms shaped like little penises, are protective—the idea is that they either summon forth one's virility or amuse the evil spirit in question.

Wearing small mojo bags of rue (or rue mixed with other protective herbs) can also be useful.

In each case these charms are reflective, protective, or they cause amusement. Almost of them can be blessed as well, adding an extra level of protection (well, *all* of them can be blessed, but depending on what type of clergy is doing the blessing, they may look askance at some of these items—though again, this is relative to locale).

Personally, I think your best bet is to stay energetically aware and clean. That way you'll be more likely to notice quickly when something is amiss around you. If you're intimately conscious and aware of your energy patterns, you'll notice almost immediately when they're disrupted. Now, malicious spirits can be tricky, and they tend to want to hide. Once you know the name of what is afflicting you, it gives you power over the thing. It puts you in control. That's something that many malignant creatures will try with all their might to avoid. So, there can be a mental component to this; a fogginess. You may not even consider the evil eye in yourself whereas you would with anyone else. Be aware of these things and when in doubt, act as if.

Sometimes I half suspect that many of these charms are really a way of warning the spirit of *malocchio* that we're ready for it. We see you. We know your name. Come here at your own risk (sort of like the ADT signs you can put outside your house to warn off burglars).

By the way, the beads and charms have to be seen. I was once warned that it's not enough just to have them, they have to be worn in such a way that they can be *seen*, ostensibly by the malevolent spirit. Let it know you're ready for it and know exactly what steps to take to drive it off. Think of it like a bully: challenge them and often they melt away.

So, my general apotropaic solution is to cleanse regularly energetically, practice those exercises (grounding, centering, shielding), maintain a regular prayer and/or devotional practice, and wear some sort of charm to ward this off. Be aware of the people in your life and trust your gut instinct. I've never diagnosed the evil eye without the client knowing immediately from whence it came. I've never recognized that I've been hit with it, without knowing immediately from whence it came. Be aware of the people in your life and maintain good boundaries. The cleaner you are energetically, the more aware and mindful of your psychic and energetic "hygiene," the harder it is for something like this to take purchase.

Miscellaneous Reading

Abu-Rabia, Aref. "The Evil Eye and Cultural Beliefs Among the Bedouin Tribes of the Negev, Middle East." *Folklore* 116:3 (2005): 241-254.

Berry, Veronica. "Neapolitan Charms Against the Evil Eye." *Folklore* 79:4 (1968): 250-256.

Burne, Charlotte S. "Charm Against the Evil Eye." *Folklore* 13:2 (1902): 202.

Di Grigoli, Veronica. *How to Protect Yourself Against the Evil Eye*. CreateSpace, 2015.

Di Stasi, Lawrence. *Mal Occhio (Evil Eye): The Underside of Vision*. North Point Press, 1983.

Dundes, Alan. *The Evil Eye: A Casebook*. University of Wisconsin Press, 1992.

Elworthy, Frederick Thomas. *The Evil Eye: The Classic Account of an Ancient Superstition*. Dover, 2004.

Gamache, Henri. *Protection Against Evil*. Raymond Publishing, 1969.

Hildburgh, W. L. "Cowrie Shells as Amulets in Europe." *Folklore* 53:4 (1942): 178-195.

Pieroni, Andrea and Maria Elena Giusti. "Ritual Botanicals Against the Evil Eye in Tuscany, Italy." *Economic Botany* 56:2 (2002): 201-203.

Reicher, Sophie. *Spiritual Protection: A Safety Manual for Energy Workers, Healers and Psychics*. New Page Books, 2010.

Thompson, M.S. "Notes from Greece and the Aegean. Evil Eye Charms." *Folklore* 19:4 (1908): 469-470.

Yronwode, Catherine. *Hoodoo Herb and Root Magic: A Materia Magica of African-American Conjure.* Lucky Mojo Curio Company, 2002.

About the Author

Galina Krasskova is a Heathen priest, vitki, and Northern Tradition shaman and has been a practicing magus for nearly thirty years. She is the founder of the *comitatus pilae cruentae* tradition and blogs regularly at http://krasskova.wordpress.com.

Made in United States
Troutdale, OR
07/18/2023

11393719R00030